The Descent

Mary W

BookLeaf Publishing

Presentation by *BookLeaf Publishing*

Web: www.bookleafpub.com

E-mail: info@bookleafpub.com

ISBN: 9789357214322

First edition 2023

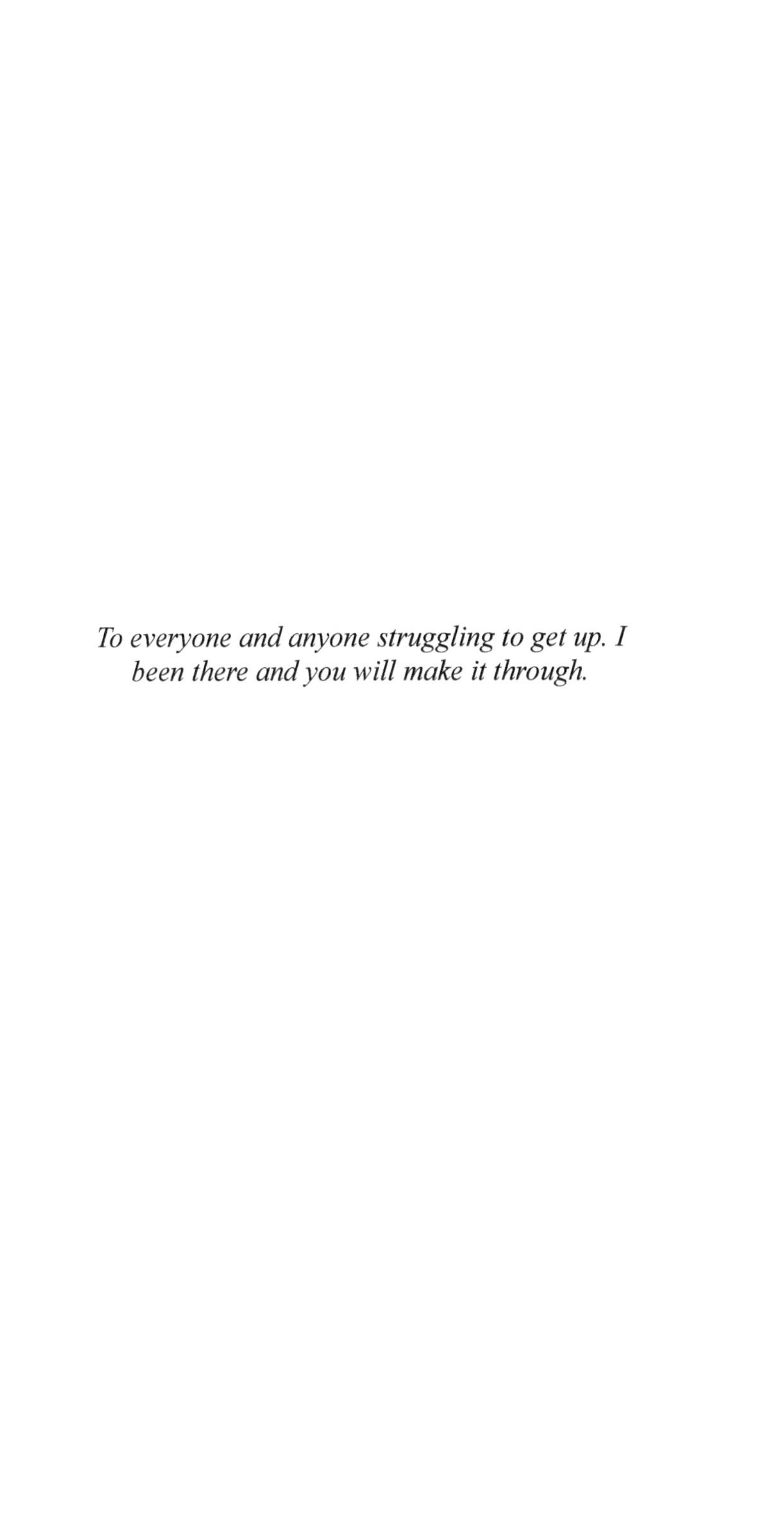

To everyone and anyone struggling to get up. I been there and you will make it through.

ACKNOWLEDGEMENT

Thanks to my friends for listening to me read my work out loud (Olivia, you litz were so helpful in writing this particular book). Thanks to my dad for always being supportive no matter what. Thanks to everyone who picks this book up and finds it great, horrible, or even mediocre. It still means the world. And thanks to Book Leaf Publishing for doing this! :)

PREFACE

Before reading, please note that this book has references to suicidal tendencies, mental illness, and death. If you are suffering from suicidal thoughts or with your mental illness, please reach out to the mental health charity and hotline, Samaritans:

📞: 116 123
💬: text SHOUT to 85258
🖥 : www.samaritans.org

You are not and never will be alone.

The Descent is a fiction based on reality. It pulls from my own experience as its foundation, but adds on dreams and stories that exist outside of my own world to round out the experience of depression and anxiety. Mental health feels like a lonely and personal process which is why every "poem" is written as diary entries. And what could be more personal than one's own journal.

The poems follow a downward spiral that sometimes doesn't make exact sense and may not feel specifically linear because it isn't. Falling deeper into mental illness isn't a straightforward process and I wanted to capture this from one poem to the next. Even though, sometimes it seems like the narrator is "doing okay," if you read the first poem to the last, it is clear they never were.

If you are struggling with mental illness, I hope you can relate to the Descent and see that one day things can improve. If you are not facing mental illness, I hope these poems help you understand it a little more.

And to everyone who has picked this up, thank you for reading. I truly appreciate it.

xoxo,
Mary

I loved life today.

Dear Diary,

I loved life today.

I felt the sun and the wind caress my face in soft circles.

Why doesn't anyone tell you how good it feels to just lay in the grass?

To feel the prickly sting from the tip of a blade followed by that satisfying itch that reminds you, you're alive and there and can still feel.

Why doesn't anyone explain that to not feel this way is not the norm?

To not feel the sun nor the grass means you are only halfway here.

Halfway gone.
Halfway out.
Half.

But today, I loved life because I could feel and there's nothing that could ever be as good in comparison.

Not the best drug.
The most loving hug.
The most scenic view.

Nothing.

I couldn't stop daydreaming.

Dear Diary,

I couldn't stop daydreaming.

I don't dream at night anymore. I wonder if it feels the same.

The way you feel unattached to the Earth and in another realm that is fully crafted for you.

There is love and happiness and joy. All the things that you want in reality, but are always just out of reach in the real world.

Like a book on the highest shelf. If you get on your tippy toes, you just might be able to touch the spine. But you can never get it down.

I want to daydream every day.

I just wish it could continue into the night.

What do you call this feeling?

Dear Diary,

What do you call this feeling?

When seeing her face makes you smile with no end?

Hearing her voice makes your heart beat a little faster?

Touching her hands makes you feel like a brand new person?

Is this…

Infatuation?

Obsession?

Happiness?

Should there be more questions than answers when all you feel is a definitive sureness?

I want to spend all my time wrapped up in her. I want to lay in bed and talk about nothing all day. Tell her my deepest secrets. My stupidest memories.

I want to look at her for hours without saying a word and just know that what we have exists. Is real. Is something you can touch and hold. Is reality.

I finally feel like my two feet are on the ground when I'm in her presence. Like all the sadness that swirls inside of my stomach is gone.

Is this what will finally save me?

I thought everything would change because of her.

Dear Diary,

If love is the answer, then what does it mean that I still feel empty most days?

I thought everything would change because of her.

That the joy she brings to my life would cure the darkness always sitting in my periphery.

I don't understand what I'm doing wrong.

I am a good girlfriend.

She is a phenomenal partner.

I am tender and caring.

She is patient and loving.

We are everything.

But I still feel nothing.

Who told me that love is the answer? Because it
doesn't feel like it.

Well, maybe I wasn't asking the right question.

Why does each day feel like a more hollow version of the other?

Dear Diary,

Why does each day feel like a more hollow version of the other?

A skeleton copy of the things that happened before.

Wake up.
Wash.
Rinse.
Work.
Sleep.
Repeat.

It feels like a never ending ferris wheel. I'm supposed to be excited, maybe even happy, but I stopped smiling 10 minutes ago.

And all I wanna do is get off.

Stop moving for 1 second so I can focus on one thing. Hold on to it for one minute longer before moving on to the next step of the laundry list.

Where am I on the list anyway?

Am I hidden in the second between waking up and getting up?

Bundled underneath work responsibilities?

Or am I not there at all? Locked away somewhere else while this body keeps doing what "it's supposed to do."

Or maybe this is me?

The constant exhaustion. Disassociation. Lack of fulfillment.

Did I ever leave at all?

Exhaustion.

Dear Diary,

Exhaustion won today.

Monsters Incorporated.

Dear Diary,

I can't stop crying after watching Monsters Inc.

Sully loved Boo enough to save her, return her home, AND came back to visit her years later.

It's the epitome of love.

To never forget someone. To always come back.

They're like a family.

Boo.

Sully.

Mike.

Eating together. Spending time. Taking care of one another.

I can't stop crying thinking about all of them together.

Why is this movie hitting me where it hurts?

Is it because I am the Sully? The overloving monster with an outrageous plan and too big heart.

Or am I the Mike? The skeptical friend who will still help out even though they're not sure the plan will work.

Maybe I'm the Boo? Just here for a good time and full of love for everyone else.

Sometimes I feel like I could be all three. And that might not be a bad thing.

Slice of life.

Dear Diary,

I just had a pizza party.

Just like the old school ones from primary
school when everyone had perfect attendance.

This time, everyone was just a little older and
we weren't celebrating our commitment to
education. We were just celebrating being.
Existing in each other's presence with something
that tastes good.

Could the true meaning of life be gathering
people you love together for no reason other
than just because you love each other?

Not because it's Christmas.

Not because it's a birthday.

Just because?

It sounds right, but why doesn't it happen more?

I won't question it today, because all I feel is happiness snuggled up with my friends and holding this slice of life.

I don't know if I've ever been in love, but I think I love pizza parties.

My brain has other plans.

Dear Diary,

She made me whole again.

How can I be so okay in her embrace when I feel so upside down outside of it?

Do I just need her to hug me and never let go?

Can hugs be the cure for depression?

For anxiety?

Even just a bad day?

I'll take that at this point.

Because I want to smile every day for her.

For her soft lips.

Almond eyes.

Perfect face.

Soft hips.

I want to smile for her every single day.

My brain just has other plans.

Bcd.

Dear Diary,

I couldn't get out of bed.

I think it and I are one and the same now.

I've been laying here on my back for so long
that I can't remember if I have something to do.

Is it Monday?

Is it Friday?

Is it a holiday?

I couldn't tell you.

I won't check my phone.

It'll hurt more to know if I missed a meeting.

Missed a deadline.

Missed a birthday.

Missed her call.

Missed their messages.

Missed.

I'll stay here for now.

It will be better tomorrow.

 or ?

Dear Diary,

Am I just a little kid hiding in the skin of a 29 year old?

Honestly, if you told me I wasn't 8 years old right now, I'd struggle to believe you, because aren't I just in the same place?

Still single…

Still confused about what I want to do with my life…

Still freaking out about things I can't control…

I think adulthood is fake and the real fact is:

We never grow up.

We just get better at pretending we did.

Who was the world made for?

Dear Diary,

Who was the world made for?

With my dark skin, 4c hair, gay heart, anxiety, depression, uterus, I don't think it was for me.

I can barely make it through a 5 day work week without falling asleep. I can't leave my house without racism, homophobia, sexism on my tails. I can't stop getting sick every 2 weeks. But I have to keep going because I don't really have a choice in this game called capitalism.

In an ideal world, I would take a sick year.

Finally win over my list of "ailments"

Long Covid
Anxiety
Depression
Chronic Fatigue
Being a woman
Being Black

Being Queer
Being outspoken

But is this really the list of things wrong with
me? It's a mix of how shitty I feel on the inside
with how shitty the outside makes me feel. My
existence and my illnesses feel like they have
become one and the same.

Being a woman with periods means Long Covid
is worse when I have them.

Being Black means my anxiety flares up when a
Karen is ready to tell me why I don't belong.

Being Queer ratchets up my depression because
many people I love will never accept me
because I can't choose who my heart wants.

Being outspoken means asking again and again
for the same thing, bringing on more and more
fatigue from being faced with the choice that's
not a choice to keep asking or never get justice.

I don't need to cure my Blackness, Womanhood,
Queerness, Fight for equity. Perhaps, I don't
need to cure my long covid, anxiety, depression,
or fatigue. The latter are symptoms of existing in

a world not made for all of the former. The parts that make me, me. That makes us, us.

So who was the world made for? It wasn't for me. It probably isn't for us. Potentially not even for you.

Capitalism.

Dear Diary,

Why did they decide it should be the "haves" and the "have-nots"?

Why couldn't it be the "haves" and the "have-mores"?

Because I don't care how much more is yours as long as everyone has something.

Help?

Dear Diary,

How do you ask for help?

I don't think I ever learned how.

I don't cry anymore when people die.

Dear Diary,

I don't cry anymore when people die.

Is something wrong with me?

It's not like I don't have the crying gene. I cry about everything. When someone raises their voice. If a dog trips on its leash. If a Disney movie is mildly sad.

My nickname growing up was "baby" because I could never stop tears from flowing. They always came. But now there's only one exception.

I don't cry anymore when people die.

I remember the day that broke me. Or was it more than one? A slow trail of days that felt like one long afternoon that was actually made up of weeks. A hospital bed. A ventilator. A racist nurse. A fighting family.

The first crack was her waving hand as I went to work.

What's more important? Capitalism or family? I never knew how to make that choice. She said she was okay. She wasn't. She never was. That was goodbye. Because she was half gone after that.

Weeks long coma.

 Another crack.

She woke up once. I was at work.

She woke up again. I was there. Watching her for the night. She couldn't speak. Only scan my face, begging for water with a slight move of her lips. Water. I begged the nurse to give it to her.

Crack.

She begged me for help. I begged them for help. They said no. Medical speak.

Crack.

Stern faces. My tears. Her disappointment. I never saw her awake again.

Weeks of a coma. Surgery options. Family discussions. Too young to understand or take part or help. Arguments. Their tears. No. My tears? Family's faces blurred in saltwater. I still had to go to work.

Then the waiting. Waiting for her to get better? Waiting for her to die?

I'll never know the answer, but it wasn't the first one.

Pasta.

Dear Diary,

Happiness is a five letter word named pasta.

Or maybe it's a six letter word named bestie.

I'm not sure if you can measure happiness in carbonara, but when you're eating with your best friend, it feels like the sky's the limit.

Maybe there's something to this thing called life if you have someone by your side. Maybe things are just a little brighter because someone is there to hold your hand while you're crying. Feed you pasta and laugh with you.

Friendship is the utmost form of romance.

I think that's the best lesson I've learned today.

Does everything have to be a question?

Dear Diary,

I hate that everything is a question.

It's like I don't have the answer to anything in my life nor the control to find it.

I refuse to keep being so confused about the state of my own world. Of my inner being.

How dare I not understand her.

How dare she be so complex after so many years.

It doesn't make sense that life doesn't get easier as you get older.

It feels like it's a formula, a mathematical equation that I learned in middle school, but definitely forgot how to solve.

I'll turn in the homework with a big question mark and an empty space.

Because I can't figure it out.

I might be done trying to.

Stay.

Dear Diary,

I want to stay.

I want to stay and fight and try and heal and beat
this.

I have so much life to live and I can't believe
how much I've missed.

How I didn't see…

The downward spiral.

The continuous fall.

The descent.

I wish it was someone's job to look at people
and say "You're not okay" and then sign you up
for therapy, a psychology appointment, and
drive you there.

If it was someone else's job, then maybe I would
have figured this out much earlier.

I would have gotten the help I needed sooner.

But as they say: it's better late than never.

And I may be late, but I'm never giving up.

Writing saved my life.

Dear Diary,

Writing saved my life.

Ironically, I cannot put into words the exact way it did it, but you'll have to believe me.

Being able to put my racing thoughts down on the page has done something to those thoughts that I could have never done on my own.

It showed my darkest feelings.

My brightest dreams.

My overwhelming anxious clouds that spin around and around in my mind.

Paper made the good and the bad real.

They made them inescapable.

They made me truthful.

It's hard to lie to yourself when you start
writing.

And I am thankful for that.

www.ingramcontent.com/pod-product-compliance
Lightning Source LLC
LaVergne TN
LVHW051241200726
843510LV00011B/1634